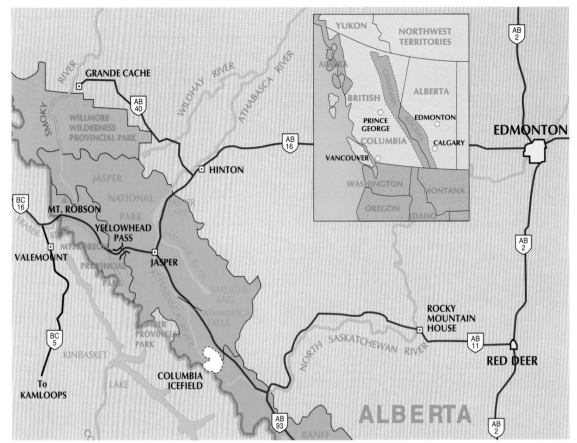

Jasper National Park

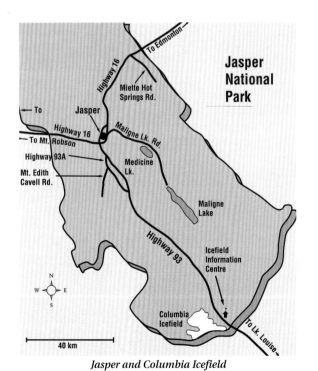

Jasper and Columbia Icefield

Elk   (photo: D. Schmidt)

Jasper & *The Columbia Icefield*

An Altitude Publishing Pictorial Book
with photographs by Lee Simmons

Athabasca River

The Icefields Parkway is by far the most spectacular route through the Canadian Rockies. Winding along the Sunwapta Valley floor, it follows the Sunwapta River to a number of breathtaking viewpoints.

From the Parkway, one of the first impressive sights is the Athabasca Glacier, which extends from the massive Columbia Icefield. Emerging from this eery landscape, the Icefields Parkway continues past Mt. Wilcox (2,884 m) and the lovely Endless Chain Ridge, until it reaches the breathtaking Sunwapta Falls. Amid the roar of the falls, bighorn sheep often graze placidly at roadside, delighting visitors with a closeup view of their heavy, curled horns.

16.9 km north of Sunwapta Falls, the Goats and Glaciers viewpoint provides a stunning perspective of the Athabasca Valley. Here, agile mountain goats are often seen licking the sulphur-rich glacial sediment in the riverbanks.

Continuing past the lovely Mt. Edith Cavell (3,363 m), the Parkway approaches Athabasca Falls, where the river skips over a stone outcropping before it plunges headlong to the bottom of the falls, 23 m below.

The Icefields Parkway terminates at Jasper, an alpine wilderness of crystalline lakes, rugged peaks and panoramic vistas.

Previous page: Athabasca Glacier at the Columbia Icefield

Looking east along Connaught Drive

Connaught with The Whistlers in the background

CN Train and Pyramid Mountain

Jasper Information Centre in downtown Jasper

Pyramid Lake and Pyramid Mountain

*J*asper National Park invariably takes first-time visitors by surprise. With its rugged wilderness and friendly, welcoming community, it is a magical blend of natural diversity and rural charm.

At 10, 878 km^2, Jasper is the largest of the Rocky Mountain national parks, and its recreational opportunities, as well as its scenic attractions, are virtually limitless. The footpaths around Pyramid Lake are among the 1,000 maintained hiking trails in the park, and some are frequented by horseback riders. The lakes, for which

Horseback riding in Jasper

Pyramid Lake with canoes

Rocky Mountain Lily

Jasper is famous, are a veritable playground for paddlers, fishermen and—on Pyramid Lake—even motor boats.

In the spring and summer months, Jasper is in full bloom. Its lake shores and trailsides are graced each year with an abundance of brilliant wildflowers.

Lac Beauvert and Jasper Park Lodge

Jasper Park Lodge with Old Man Mountain in the background

*I*n the 935 m of the Jasper Tramway's spectacular climb, it traverses montane, sub-alpine and alpine ecoregions, all of which support a great diversity of plant life and animals. The view from the upper terminal is nothing short of breathtaking—alpine lakes are scattered in the embrace of the surrounding mountain ranges, and the Athabasca and Miette River valleys wind serenely along their courses.

Even from this vantage point, the rustic and luxurious Jasper Park Lodge, on the shore of Lac Beauvert, is lovely.

Opposite page: Jasper Tramway with the town of Jasper far below

Maligne Canyon viewed from bridge

Maligne Canyon viewpoint

Maligne Canyon, the deepest and longest canyon in the Canadian Rockies, was formed when the Athabasca River carved its way through the limestone bedrock that lay in its path. According to one early visitor, "any other canyon is like a crack in a teacup."

Six bridges span Maligne Canyon, and visitors can walk its entire length from the sixth bridge. From the Maligne Canyon Teahouse, high above the water's incessant rush, many of the area's highlights are revealed. But the secrets of this 11,000-year-old canyon are not to be heard in the river's roar. Rather, the canyon's past is contained in its rocks, where fossils of snail- and squid-like creatures lie frozen in time amid petrified coral.

Opposite page: Bridges straddle the steep walls of Maligne Canyon

Maligne Lake Boat House

Moss Campion

Opposite page: Medicine Lake
Following page: Early morning at Spirit Island on Maligne Lake

Maligne River, which is fed by Maligne Lake, was named by a Belgian missionary to describe its furious, headlong rush. *Maligne,* or "wicked" in French, seems incongruous with this tranquil, glacier-fed lake.

By far the largest natural lake in the Canadian Rockies, it is 22 km long and has an area of 21 km^2. Visitors can reach the far end on foot or by renting a boat for a leisurely paddle past Spirit Island.

The area is replete with moss campion, a hardy alpine plant. Despite its delicate appearance, it grows close to the ground in wide-open spaces, and can exist on very thin, nutrient-poor soil. Its low stature allows it to take advantage of sunlight while being sheltered from the wind.

Grizzly bear and cub   (photo: D. Schmidt)

Indian Paintbrush

Sunset at Spirit Island on Maligne Lake

Mt. Edith Cavell

Black bear   (photo: D. Schmidt)

Mt. Edith Cavell is Jasper's signature landmark. Looming impressively on the skyline, its vertical face acts as a snowfence, which piles snow onto its less steep inclines below to create Cavell Glacier. This phenomenon can be observed more closely from Path of the Glacier Trail, which begins at the mountain's base.

Mt. Edith Cavell was named after a martyred war hero, Edith Louisa Cavell, who was executed by German forces during World War I for having assisted the escape of allied prisoners of war.

Opposite page: Angel Glacier hangs on the side of Mt. Edith Cavell

Bighorn sheep

Diverted from its course by a glacial moraine, the Sunwapta River tumbles down Sunwapta Falls before it is reunited with the Athabasca River.

Bighorn rams convene at high elevations during the fall rutting season, when the dominant ram must defend his right to mate with the ewes in his harem. When rams duel, they charge toward each other and meet with a thunderous crash.

The ram's age can be estimated by counting the rings on one of its horns. Each light and dark band together—called an *annulus*—represents one year of growth.

Sunwapta Falls Resort

Opposite page: Sunwapta Falls

Tangle Falls at the Columbia Icefield

Opposite page: Athabasca Falls

A mountain goat enjoys a view of the Athabasca Glacier

A Brewster Snocoach on Athabasca Glacier

*T*he Columbia Icefield is an impressive remnant of the forces that molded the landscape of the Canadian Rockies.

Glacier ice is formed when, year after year, the snow that falls in the winter accumulates rather than melting. Eventually, the compressed snow becomes ice. Moving under its own weight, it leaves a path in its wake, along with rock rubble or glacial moraines. These moraines can form dammed depressions in the earth in which water gathers, resulting in a lake or its smaller version, a tarn.

Opposite page: The view from Goats and Glaciers Viewpoint
Following page: Columbia Icefield Centre

The Columbia Icefield Centre

The Columbia Icefield Centre patio

Glacier Gallery, Columbia Icefield Centre

*T*here are two ways to explore the fascinating world of the Columbia Icefield: by taking a guided walk on the toe of the glacier, or by riding a Brewster Snocoach onto Athabasca Glacier. Either way, you will uncover the mysteries of this frozen hinterland. Trained mountain guides help ensure your safety during your exploration, and the knowledgeable tour guides aboard the Snocoaches explain why the ice is blue, the meaning of "watermelon snow," and the adaptations of the animals that survive here in winter, when the temperature often drops below -40°C.

Snocoaches, too, have been adapted over the years to minimize the ecological impact of our presence in this rugged-but-fragile ecosystem. Today, these safe and comfortable, 56-passenger vehicles provide a unique opportunity to step onto the ice at the centre of the retreating Athabasca Glacier.

Opposite page: A Brewster Snocoach with Mt. Andromeda in the background

A Brewster Snocoach with Mt. Andromeda in the background

A Brewster Snocoach with the icefall at the head of Athabasca Glacier

Snocoaches leaving the turn around area on Athabasca Glacier

Mt. Andromeda and Athabasca Glacier

*A*n Icefield, from which glaciers flow outward in more than one direction, covers the Continental Divide between Kicking Horse Pass and Athabasca Pass. The vast Columbia Icefield's meltwater feeds three of the largest river systems in Canada: the Columbia River, the Athabasca and McKenzie rivers, and the North Saskatchewan, Saskatchewan and Nelson rivers. The meltwater makes its way down these river systems to the Pacific, Arctic and Atlantic oceans, respectively.

Following page:
Looking south on the Icefields Parkway with
Mt. Athabasca and Mt. Andromeda in the background